Reminds Me of Sunshine

Jazmine Baehr

BookLeaf Publishing

India | USA | UK

Presentation by *BookLeaf Publishing*

Web: www.bookleafpub.com

E-mail: info@bookleafpub.com

ISBN: 9789357445542

First edition 2022

DEDICATION

For Nana

ACKNOWLEDGEMENT

I'd like to acknowledge BookLeaf Publishing for making one of my childhood dreams come true.

PREFACE

Various poems in this book will depict my experience of living with Bipolar Disorder...these experiences are unique to me and do not encase all the ways depression and/or mania may present themselves.

Cement shoes

Lying fallow on the ocean floor; cement shoes
fastened tightly

The waters edge just beyond my reach

You call out why don't you just break free

... because then I will truly know what it feels
like to drown.

Books

I was asked recently what I am grateful for, without pause I exclaimed books.

Naturally I was met by a sea of bewildered looks because even though they are asking you a question you're not supposed to answer honestly.

You're supposed to say some bullshit cliche like oh my family or the air in my lungs...I'm not a monster of course I'm grateful for those as well...

But books are my first love, reading is quite possibly the most beautiful escape I have yet to know.

To be able to shed my own self and dive deep into the safe space that forms in between lines on the page

To exchange my identity for another if even for just a brief moment in time.

It's as if reading is the closest to magic most people will ever achieve in their lifetime

Fences

It genuinely perplexes me when a person claims they just want to mend fences.

Mending fences otherwise known as I don't want to take responsibility for my actions but this situation is making my life a little less comfortable so let's just move on.

What good does mending fences do when you have destroyed foundations where entire worlds once stood?

When you have doused the whole damn situation in gasoline and set it ablaze and now you've returned to nothing but ashes.

No matter how many fences you mend around a graveyard it doesn't bring the bodies inside back to life.

Toothpaste

Watching the news or scrolling on social media as people continuously hurl insults and jabs at one another I am reminded of a lesson I was taught in kindergarten.

I remember on this specific day my teacher covered the tables in plastic wrap and handed each child a tube of toothpaste.

We all looked at one another a little confused, excited and just a bit worried because it was the minty kind grownups used unlike that watermelon flavored one by Colegate that basically every child used.

The teacher then directed us to squeeze the toothpaste out of the tubes and onto the table.

With our eager little hands we squeezed every last bit out of our tubes as we squealed with joy and giggles because well....it was fun.

The teacher then said okay now I want you to put the toothpaste back into the tubes...a silent panic washed over the room as we then frantically attempted to return the displaced toothpaste.

Unsuccessful, we one after another began to crescendo in meltdowns until the teacher brought the room to a silent calm and explained that we must consider the consequences of our actions, not just the moment we were currently in.

Words thrust into the universe cannot be unspoken; and we have surely realized by now that what happens on the internet will forever remain. Much like how toothpaste cannot be put back into its tube.

At such young ages we teach children that their actions have consequences yet adults are so quick to lash out without recognizing the gravity of our words, and energy of our actions.

Blood in the water

Nervous, always nervous; never showing but always there.

Right underneath the skin flowing through my veins with each loud thud of my heart, pounding in my ears.

Panicked so very panicked but a cool demeanor is a requirement if you don't want to allude to the thoughts ping ponging off the inside of your skull.

Hands are shaky just blame it on the coffee and redbull people will chuckle and tell you what a time senior year of college is to be alive.

They'll ask you repetitive questions about the future when you know for a fact that you can't even be sure of what you'll have for dinner tonight which is a whole six hours away.

Scared; perhaps even terrified but god knows you can't make up your mind on how you feel;

too many options in feelings, in food, in life
after college. Overwhelmed feel like you're
drowning.

Internally let the options rampage while
nodding, keeping a pleasant smile, and your
answers vague for safety of course.

Everyone knows sharks can smell blood in the
water.

Grounding

Just count to ten it'll all be okay...

One

Mind racing; okay grounding feet flat on the
floor fingers spread wide as they can go against
the cool wall.

Two

Take inventory of how you are feeling; chest
feels tight, panicking about how your fucking
your entire schedule for this meltdown.

Three

Feels like each nerve ending is on fire. Every
little ache and pain is like white hot lightning
rampaging as if using your body like a racetrack.

Four

Suddenly remember how pathetic this must be to watch ; a stark contrast to the image of strength people have thrust upon you.

Five

Halfway through now and you still don't feel any better in fact you feel worse from when you started.

Six

Overstimulated, too loud, too bright everything seems blurred which is made worse by the stinging sensation in your nose that signals oncoming tears.

Seven

Tears begin first slow sniffles then all at once into full body sobs; the sound of your heartbeat in your ears begins to recede.

Eight

Chest starts to loosen breathing slightly easier,
regain the ability to stand up straight without the
support of the wall.

Nine

Collect yourself, tears subside; you're prepared
for this, fix your hair, pull the frozen spoons out
of the freezer the puffiness of crying will soon
be gone. Fix your makeup, remember to thank
god for waterproof mascara.

Ten

External signs now hidden away return to your
schedule; you're late, glance in the mirror before
you go to ensure no trace has gone unhidden.

Count to ten they say you'll feel better; if that's
true why do I still feel like I want to die?

Demons in disguise

Have you ever stared into the eyes of a person you once loved and realized that they were no longer in there?

Instead you've been met by cold, dark, and unforgiving eyes that send chills down your spine when you meet their gaze.

Studied the features of a face you've known so well but now the expressions just don't match the words coming out of its mouth.

It's hard when you only have a soul to bury because the mortal vessel is being paraded around by some demon in disguise

Emotions

Emotions are finicky, they are messy, and often unpredictable and while most people like to think the contrary they are almost completely out of our control.

If you're really good you can control the outward expression of each emotion but not the emotion itself.

We live in a society that puts down those of us who experience our emotions out loud...specifically the negative ones.

Society has made us into the human equivalents of champagne bottles that have been shaken and are about to blow at any moment's notice.

Emotions are just like the world that surrounds us...they are meant to be experienced.

BT

I am drunk on gin and unattainable dreams;
come sunrise I will be filled with nothing but
regret but for now I am happy.

Your name is on my phone with the little red
heart emoji next to it because I never changed it.
I always hoped you'd change instead.

Over a thousand miles away and you're
whispering sweet nothings to me because you're
drunk and you're turned on by the sound of my
voice.

I am easily won over by your words; I slip away
from the party to make familiar concessions.

Come sunrise I will be filled with nothing but
regret but for now I am happy.

Do it for yourself

People always do things for other people; but never themselves.

Half hearted attempts and a head full of airbrushed fantasies created by the media.

So wrapped up in seeking the approval and acceptance of others that we forget that each one of us is a magnificent piece of art.

Forget the opinions of others; show up for yourself because you deserve it.

Note to my future self

Dear future self -

You are a miracle, did you know that?

You've pulled thorns out of your own paws, knives out of your own back and you still manage to greet the world with curiosity rather than condemnation.

You have spent most of your life teetering on the edge of a cliff deciding whether or not it was worth it to stay; all while convincing the spectators that it was some circus-like performance.

You've woken up day after day and chosen to fight because even when you couldn't see the bright side you were sure it was hiding out there somewhere.

You are becoming everything five year old you wanted to be.

You are already something thirteen year old you thought she would never be...

You are reading this poem and that alone says it all.

Reminds me of sunshine

We've been made to believe that red is the color of love when it should be yellow.

Yellow like the Del's lemonade you drink while wandering around the late summer fairs in New England.

Yellow like running through fields of sunflowers as they follow the sun throughout the day.

Yellow like the sun room in the house on 219 where I laid on the floor and counted the ladybugs that had been attracted by the bright paint that adorned the walls.

Yellow like the sun I bathe in as it peeks through the clouds for the first time in days; even if its presence is fleeting.

Sadness sells

The world expects poets to be sad; everyone
wants to talk about how sex sells but no one
wants to admit that so does sadness.

TV has romanticized mental illness to a point
that people without it think it's a selling point; a
schtick to make yourself more interesting.

People go wide-eyed with a twisted sort of
excitement when I talk about living with Bipolar
like they are small children hearing about Santa
Claus for the very first time.

Vain attempts to conceal their desire to try on
my raw emotions like halloween costumes; so
entirely consumed that they forget that my pain
is real.

Hasn't it ever occurred to you that I am so
fucking lucky that I have survived to tell you
this story?

Passages

Write it down, I'm sure you won't feel it later...

I'm a glutton for punishment; I hold onto my old journals and when I am feeling especially low I go hunting for passages that will make me feel worse.

They tell you to write a letter when you are feeling strong emotions and then burn it because emotions are just in the moment.

That couldn't be more wrong; as I run my fingers over the pages I nearly burn myself because they are still very much a live fire.

Into thin air

Deeply inhale and become one with the floor.

On the exhale try to visualize your belly button touching your spine.

Feel yourself start to melt like a popsicle in the hot summer sun.

Perhaps if you try hard enough you'll vanish into thin air.

Electricity

Live wires under my skin;

Electricity ripping through my veins; sitting still
becomes nearly impossible but I wouldn't want
to bring unnecessary attention to myself.

No one would understand, so I suffer in silence
and pray the current finds their way out soon.

Silence

Alone in your apartment trying to distract yourself from how quiet it is; no one ever told you that silence could be this loud.

Live wires under your skin keep you from sitting still for too long so sleep is definitely out of the question.

Music, books, and even writing seem overwhelming to a point of despair so at last you are forced to focus on the rabbit hole in your mind.

Wrapped up in your own thoughts, some real, some made up but you haven't slept in three days so the line between the two is pretty blurry.

The war rages on; you try to get control but it's a losing battle. All you can think of now is how much you miss the silence.

Little white pill

It's 10am, the alarm on your phone goes off, you go running, little white pill needs to be taken at the same time every day to maximize effectiveness.

Funny how society's view on drugs shifts when you put the word prescription in front.

Six weeks ago you were nearly ready to skin yourself in order to grab hold of the electric current running rampant making it impossible to sleep, to focus, to function.

A ticking time bomb waiting to explode because the wind is hitting your face incorrectly; because someone looked at you wrong, or even just dropping your pencil.

Now you can sit still again, taste food, listen to a song the entire way through.

All because of one little white pill

Floating

There is this space in between depression and mania

it's the smell outside after a thunderstorm

it's the first deep breath of fresh air when you reach the mountain top

it's like floating gently in the ocean where it seems almost like nothing could go wrong, but if it did you'd be able to handle it.

Smiley face

When you've been down for so long you forget
how everything other than sadness feels.

I absentmindedly drew a smiley face in the dust
on the elevator door.

For days I brightened just for a few seconds
every time I saw it.

Although it may not seem like much I was
reminded that my muscles still remembered
what it felt like to be happy.

Daylight

Shrouded in the darkness,

The dawn has evaded me for so long.

I almost forgot what it felt like to feel the
daylight;

It is glorious.